DATE DUE

			PRINTED IN U.S.A.

Animal Hospital
Rescuing Urban Wildlife

Julia Coey

FIREFLY BOOKS

A Firefly Book

Published by Firefly Books Ltd. 2015
Copyright © 2015 Firefly Books Ltd.
Text copyright © 2015 Toronto Wildlife Centre

Toronto
Wildlife
Centre

First printing

Publisher Cataloging-in-Publication Data (U.S.)
Coey, Julia, 1977- .
Animal hospital : rescuing urban wildlife / Julia Coey.
[64] pages : color photographs ; cm.
Includes index.
Summary: "Animal Hospital follows the activities of an urban animal rescue facility and the efforts of the trained professionals that rescue, treat, rehabilitate and hopefully release the animals. The book explains medical triage and provides instructions on first aid steps and how to contact wildlife experts for people who discover injured animals." -- Publisher.
ISBN 13: 978-1-77085-572-4
ISBN-13: 978-1-77085-571-7 (pbk.)
1. Veterinary hospitals – Juvenile literature. I. Title.
636.0832 dc23   SF604.55C649 2015

Library and Archives Canada Cataloguing in Publication
Coey, Julia, 1977-, author
 Animal hospital : rescuing urban wildlife / Julia Coey.
Includes index.
ISBN 978-1-77085-572-4 (bound).--
ISBN 978-1-77085-571-7 (pbk.)
1. Wildlife rehabilitation--Juvenile literature. 2. Wildlife rescue--Juvenile literature. 3. Toronto Wildlife Centre--Juvenile
literature. 4. Toronto Wildlife Centre. I. Title.
SF996.45.C64 2015   j639.9'6   C2015-902974-0

Published in the United States by
Firefly Books (U.S.) Inc.
P.O. Box 1338, Ellicott Station
Buffalo, New York 14205

Published in Canada by
Firefly Books Ltd.
50 Staples Avenue, Unit 1
Richmond Hill, Ontario L4B 0A7

Cover and interior design: Hartley Millson

Printed in China

The publisher gratefully acknowledges the financial support for our publishing program by the Government of Canada through the Canada Book Fund as administered by the Department of Canadian Heritage.

Contents

Introduction

n 1992, wildlife biologist Nathalie Karvonen was working at a humane society in Toronto when she noticed a pressing need for wildlife rehabilitation services. Not only were there few options for sick, injured and orphaned wildlife, there was a lack of information and support for the people who wanted to help. In response, she founded the non-profit organization Toronto Wildlife Centre in 1992 with a handful of dedicated volunteers. What started as a basic wildlife information hotline run from a single phone is now a full service wildlife hospital and rehabilitation center with a dedicated rescue team.

Today, Toronto Wildlife Centre's hotline is run by a team of staff and volunteers who handle tens of thousands of calls each year. Over 80,000 sick, injured and orphaned wild animals representing more than 270 different species have been helped — approximately 5,000 animals a year. This is only the tip of the iceberg. All around the world, hundreds of thousands of wild animals are hurt by direct and indirect contact with humans. But wildlife rehabilitators are changing these odds.

This book tells the story of wildlife rehabilitation through the work of one of the busiest wildlife rehabilitation centers in Canada, and was made possible by Toronto Wildlife Centre's dedicated staff, volunteers and donors. Thank you for changing the world one animal at a time!

To learn more about the center and how you can help sick, injured and orphaned wild animals visit www.torontowildlifecentre.com.

Chapter 1

Understanding Wildlife Rehabilitation

A Dangerous World

In an urban landscape of concrete and cars, it sometimes seems impossible that anything wild could survive. Wild animals are creatures of the forests, the skies and the streams, not cities made of concrete and glass.

The common belief is that we have encroached on wild animals, building over their habitat and forcing them into smaller and smaller patches of green space. But is that really the case? Yes, as cities grow, forests do disappear to fuel a world bent on expansion. This is

not, however, the whole story. Some wild animals have evolved alongside humans in the urban environment, and thrive because of cities, not despite them.

In large North American cities such as New York or Toronto, commonly seen animals like squirrels and pigeons share the streets with more cautious foxes and coyotes, who travel mostly under the cover of night. Hawks and falcons sit high atop buildings and power lines, and deer move invisibly through the cityscape by sticking to green corridors. In Toronto, more than three hundred species of birds, mammals, reptiles and amphibians are roaming the streets, lakes, rivers and green spaces.

This largely unseen wild world is filled with creatures that have adapted to city living in fascinating ways. But in these close quarters, conflicts with humans are inevitable — and when they happen, it's often the wild animal that loses.

🔍 The Super-Adaptable Squirrel

Gray squirrels, which can be found in most cities across North America, have adapted very well to city living.

- They can turn their back feet 180 degrees. (Look at your own feet: now picture your toes where your heel is and your heel where your toes are!) This means they can run down trees just as quickly and easily as they run up them.
- That gorgeous bushy tail is more functional than fashionable. Squirrels use their tail to provide balance when leaping from branch to branch. It also functions as a parasol in the summer (to provide shade), an umbrella in rainstorms and a scarf in the winter. Squirrels also flick and twitch their tail to alert other squirrels of potential danger.
- Squirrels are sneaky! About 20 percent of the time, they are pretending to bury nuts and seeds, but they just dig a hole and then bury their treasure in a different place. Researchers suspect this is to trick the wild thieves, like birds or other squirrels, who may be watching.

9

Changing the Odds

Unlike zoos or wildlife sanctuaries that provide long-term homes for animals, wildlife rehabilitation centers aim to return a wild animal to its natural environment as quickly as possible. Contact with humans is kept to a minimum in order to reduce stress and to prevent habituation.

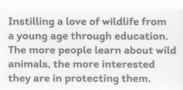

Instilling a love of wildlife from a young age through education. The more people learn about wild animals, the more interested they are in protecting them.

Wildlife rehabilitation is about changing the odds.

Wildlife rehabilitators help sick, injured and orphaned wild animals with the goal of restoring them to health and releasing them back into the wild. They are experts in the natural history of the wild animals they are helping. Some are wildlife biologists or veterinary technicians; others are animal lovers with lots of hands-on experience. Some work out of their home, while others are part of a bigger organization, like Toronto

This baby Eastern gray squirrel's leg was put in a splint and cast after an x-ray revealed a fracture.

Wildlife Centre (TWC), working alongside a wildlife veterinarian.

When asked, most wildlife rehabilitators say they feel a responsibility to help wild animals harmed by human actions. Some recall a life-changing moment when they first encountered a sick, injured or orphaned wild animal and felt helpless in the face of silent suffering.

When countries have laws and regulations that govern wildlife in captivity, wildlife rehabilitators adhere to these guidelines. Rehabilitators also rely on one another for advice, and to share new treatment protocols, rescue techniques and caging setups.

Largely volunteer-run and funded by donations, rehabilitation centers work hard to educate the public and to fulfill the goal of returning wild animals to the wild, healthy and strong. Happily, the number of wildlife rehabilitation centers (big and small) around the world has been growing for the last few decades.

An orphaned baby mink is fed a specialized formula by hand.

A mute swan is examined before being treated for zinc toxicity, which is caused by ingesting material containing zinc. Many products contain zinc, including American pennies and nails. Zinc toxicity causes liver damage.

A wildlife veterinarian checks a patient's chart before starting her exam.

Education and Awareness

Litter in the natural environment can harm wildlife in surprising ways. This young swan is not only badly injured by a discarded pop can, but is also unable to eat. Happily, the swan recovers and is released.

drive. They're injured by the fishing tackle we leave behind after our weekend trips and are poisoned by the chemicals we use in our day-to-day lives. In fact, almost everything we do affects wildlife in big or small ways.

Knowledge = Power

A big part of wildlife rehabilitation is teaching the public how to avoid putting animals at risk, and to help people resolve conflict situations without harming the animal. People accidentally create wonderful spaces for wild animals to live, eat and have babies, but then some are scared or irritated by their presence. Unsecure garbage and compost bins provide an endless buffet; forgotten holes in roofs give access to a safe nursery; backyard birdfeeders attract more than just birds. Wildlife rehabilitators educate the public whenever possible to reduce the number of animals hurt or killed by preventable hazards.

Almost all wildlife rehabilitation cases are a result of direct or indirect conflict with humans. Most people don't intentionally harm wildlife, but animals are still endangered by human behavior. They fly into the windows in our buildings or are hit by the cars we

1. Food Containers

Wild animals can get their paws and heads stuck in containers trying to reach food residue. This can prevent an animal from eating or drinking.

Prevent this: Wash out all food containers thoroughly before throwing them out or recycling them, including pop cans.

2. Kite String

Animals can get tangled in kite string left in trees, resulting in serious injuries.

Prevent this: When flying a kite, stay clear of trees and take all the string you bring (and any you find) home again.

3. Roadside Garbage

Throwing food out of car windows attracts small rodents to the roadside, which in turn attract larger species of wildlife too close to traffic!

Prevent this: Never throw garbage (even biodegradable items such as apple cores) out your car windows.

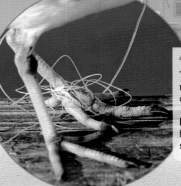

4. Fishing Line, Hooks and Lures

Tangled in the reeds, stuck on a log, resting on the bottom of the lake, discarded fishing gear can harm wildlife.

Prevent this: Don't leave any of your gear behind after a day of fishing, and when you see an abandoned line, take it with you.

5. Domed Dessert Lids

Plastic dessert cups seem to be especially tempting. Animals push their heads through the small hole at the top, but when they try to get out, the lids stays on tight.

Prevent this: Remove lids from cups and cut them up before disposal.

Treacherous Trash

One of the easiest ways we can keep wild animals safe is by watching how we dispose of our trash. Wild animals can easily hurt themselves on the things we throw away. Attracted by food scraps, animals climb into garbage bins, cut themselves on sharp cans, and squeeze their heads and paws into tight containers to access leftovers. Those fast-food dessert cup lids (the plastic domed ones) can cause serious injuries. It seems that many wild animals like ice cream treats as much as you do!

An untold number of wild animals are needlessly hurt every year because of the things we discard. Above are five easy ways to help.

Myth Busting

There's a lot of misinformation out there — and many rehabilitators' public education efforts are aimed at replacing wrong beliefs with right. Lots of people, for example, think that it's kind to trap wild animals and release them someplace else. But that's just not true. And while it may seem nice to provide food for our wild neighbors, this can actually do more harm than good.

Don't Feed the Animals!

Feeding wild animals encourages them to view humans as an easy food source and changes their foraging behavior. Ducks and geese love to eat the bread we throw to them, but it fills them up in the same way it does us. When their bellies are full of bread, they don't eat their natural nutrient-rich diet, and the unnatural

food causes digestive issues. It's also dangerous for wild animals to associate humans with food; not everyone wants to be approached by a wild animal looking for a handout!

Removing food sources, like unsecured garbage and compost bins can make your property less appealing to unwanted wildlife.

Live Trapping: A Bad Idea

It may appear that moving an animal from an urban backyard to a ravine, park or forest is a good thing, since these spaces seem more "natural." But wild animals have specific home ranges where they are adapted to living. Many city animals spend their whole lives in

Relocating wild animals can transmit diseases between animal populations.

areas smaller than half a square mile (1 sq. km), and within that range they learn where to find food, water and shelter, and how to stay safe. Being transplanted into a new, unfamiliar location — even one that looks nice to us — is stressful and bewildering. Without the necessary knowledge of their surroundings, many are unable to survive.

Most wildlife conflicts happen in the spring, summer and fall, when animals are looking hardest for shelter and for extra food to feed their babies — who are often quietly awaiting their parents return in attic nests or backyard burrows. When a parent is trapped and moved, dependent young are left behind. Without parental care, they will die.

🔍 A (True) Helping Hand

If you can't move or feed wild animals, what can you do to help? Here are a few ideas that really do work:

- *Get dirty:* Provide natural food sources and habitat by planting native bushes, trees and flowers. Shrubs (like elderberry) and conifers (like pine) provide fruit and seeds for the birds that stick around in the winter, such as American robins and black-capped chickadees.

- *Let it grow:* A garden of native grasses and wildflowers looks beautiful and doesn't need to be mowed. Long grass and bushes give baby wild animals a place to hide from predators. Low-hanging branches provide a natural ladder for fledgling birds to hop up to safety until they can fly.

- *Plant weeds, don't pull:* Reports say the number of monarch butterflies migrating to Mexico each year is in sharp decline. This decrease is linked to pesticides and to the loss of milkweed, the plant monarch larvae depend on for food. Planting wildflowers and wild grasses also supports other important pollinators like birds and bees.

Is Wildlife Rehab Important?

You've probably heard that bees help pollinate flowers, but did you know that squirrels plant trees, or that bats control insect populations? All species have important jobs in their ecosystems, some of which we're just beginning to understand.

But does saving one wild animal really make a difference? Yes! An injured female rabbit, helped and released, could have as many as three or four litters a season. Some of her babies will grow to adulthood and also reproduce. Others will be a vital food source for larger animals. Both situations create a healthy, balanced ecosystem.

But wildlife rehabilitation doesn't just help wildlife; it also helps the people who find sick, injured or orphaned animals. It can be scary and heartbreaking to see a wild animal in pain or seemingly vulnerable (like a wild baby all on its own).

Wildlife rehabilitators empower us to help when needed; they also teach us when it's better to stay away. For example, killdeer parents pretend to have a broken wing when an animal (or human) gets too close to their young. An injured bird is an easy meal and so predators are lured away from the nest. When the babies or eggs are safe, the killdeer experiences a miraculous "recovery" and flies away. To an untrained eye, it could appear that the killdeer — and, subsequently, its babies — are in need of help. Knowing that this is all part of the bird's normal behavior ensures that we aren't interfering with the natural order of things.

Also, wildlife rehabilitators are sometimes the first to spot a larger environmental problem based on the conditions of the animals they are seeing. For example, if more than one animal from the same area is found covered with oil, it could be a sign of a previously undetected spill. This information is shared with the authorities that can best deal with the situation.

Chapter 2

Rehabilitation in Action

So now you know a bit more about what wildlife rehabilitation is. But how does it work? What should you do if you find a sick, injured or orphaned wild animal? Calling for help is a great place to start.

A Call for Help

Some rehabilitation centers operate a hotline for people who are looking for help or advice on dealing with a wild animal issue. Toronto Wildlife Centre's hotline answers thousands of calls from the public every year. These calls range from emergency wildlife situations to general interest questions about wildlife.

When a wild animal does need help, hotline staff work fast to assess the situation. For dangerous or complicated situations, they send out the rescue team. Otherwise, under the direction of the hotline staff, the caller or a volunteer will safely contain and bring the animal to the center.

A headset helps hotline staff talk and type at the same time.

🔍 Killer Cats

Despite working only with wild animals, the center gets hundreds of calls every year about domestic cats. Cats prey on wild animals, and in the spring and summer, especially, many of the calls are about baby animals that have been attacked by a cat or orphaned due to a cat attack (cats are very good hunters). American research estimates that domestic cats that are allowed outdoors kill more than a million birds and small mammals each year.

How can you help? You can protect your cat, and wildlife, by keeping it inside. Outdoor cats face many dangers: predation by other animals, vehicles, human cruelty and exposure to pesticides.

The Hotline at Work

When baby rabbits leave their ground nest, they're already independent of their mother. Independent babies have fluffy fur, erect ears, are at least four inches long and can hop around quickly.

Hotlines are particularly busy in the spring and summer, when they receive thousands of calls about orphaned wild babies. Babies look so vulnerable that people instinctually want to help them. But often they are displaying normal behavior for their species and age, and the parents are nearby. Hotline staff work with callers to make sure the baby or babies actually need help before getting them in for care. The best place for wild babies is with their parents (but a wildlife rehabilitator is a close second when it comes to caregiving).

The Case of the Orphaned Baby Rabbits

Eastern cottontail rabbits dig shallow nests on the ground and cover their babies with a blanket of grasses, twigs and fur. Typically, the mother only comes to feed them at dawn and dusk. In fact, the babies are much safer when she's not

The baby rabbits cuddle together on a blanket in a cardboard box.

around. Adult rabbits have a strong scent that will attract predators, but the babies don't. Hidden under their blanket of grass, baby rabbits instinctively stay very still and are almost invisible to potential predators. However, dogs have an incredible sense of smell and can sometimes sniff out these tiny babies.

And that's exactly what happened to the rabbits pictured here. The dog's owner called Toronto Wildlife Centre and asked for advice. The hotline staff member knew exactly what questions to ask. First she made sure that the babies were in a

Fully grown eastern cottontail rabbit

safe place (either still in the nest or in a box placed in a quiet location) and had not had any contact with a cat (cat saliva contains bacteria that can cause fatal infections). She confirmed that the babies were found covered up and that the dog had not injured any of them.

Since it's normal for the mother to be absent during the day, the hotline staff member knew the bunnies might not be orphans at all. But just in case, she asked the dog's owner to perform a simple test. He laid four pieces of string over the nest in a tic-tac-toe formation. In the morning, he checked the nest to find the strings untouched. If the babies' mother had visited the nest the night before, she would have moved the strings when she uncovered and re-covered her litter. So, the babies would need to be admitted to Toronto Wildlife Centre after all.

The hotline staff member was able to provide instructions on how to safely move and transport the babies. The dog's owner was told to carefully pick up each of the babies and put them all in a box lined with a towel (they immediately cuddled together) and a heat source like a warm water bottle. Next step? Close the box lid and place it on the back seat of his car. The rabbits would be scared, the hotline staff member explained. To lessen their stress, the car radio should be turned off and the box kept closed.

Once at the center, the box was placed in the medical assessment room away from the noise of ringing phones and people talking. Soon, medical staff will examine the baby rabbits.

An eastern cottontail rabbit hides in the tall grass.

23

Assessment and Admitting

nimals arrive at rehabilitation centers in a variety of ways. Some — like the rabbits on the last page — are brought in following a hotline call. Others are transported after a rescue. But they all have something in common: their first stop is the assessment room.

 In the wild, looking healthy and strong is crucial; animals that appear sick or injured are easy prey. Even in care, their instinct is to hide any pain they are feeling and try to appear strong at all costs.

The Assessment Room

The assessment room at Toronto Wildlife Centre is like the emergency room at a hospital. All animals admitted are examined here by medical staff to determine the treatment they will need.

Assessing a wild animal is challenging. Unlike domestic animals, they don't have owners to explain the cause of their injuries, describe their symptoms or say how long they've been sick. If physical examinations (like eye exams, feeling for broken bones or assessing body condition) don't provide enough information, the animal may need to undergo laboratory diagnostics, such as blood tests for lead poisoning or anemia (low iron) and x-rays to show broken bones or foreign objects.

Let's see what happened to the Eastern cottontail babies once they were safely brought in.

Assessment, Rehab and Release

Medical staff examine the baby rabbits one at a time, leaving the others covered in the box. Wild animals are terrified by humans and highly stressed in captivity, and the less they see and are handled by people (whom they see as predators) the better.

The orphans are a little dehydrated, but otherwise healthy. They will be hand-fed formula twice a day (as often as their mother would feed them in the wild) and are given greens like clover and dandelion leaves. At this age, baby rabbits in the wild will instinctually start to supplement their mother's milk by nibbling greens. The rehab team will weigh the siblings every day to make

A young rabbit nibbles on dandelion leaves, grass and clover. Greens like these will make up most of its diet in the wild.

 Eastern cottontails are completely vegetarian. They have a unique digestive system that allows them to get nutrients from plants that are difficult to digest.

sure they are gaining weight. After about a week, hand feeding will be reduced to once a day until they are eating on their own.

When the rabbits are plump and healthy, acting like rabbits and displaying a healthy fear of people, they can be released — if the weather cooperates. To make the transition to the wild as easy as possible, they'll be released when the forecast calls for two or three days of warm dry weather.

 ## Another Myth Bites the Dust

Touching wild babies will not make their parents abandon them. Some species – like rabbits and deer – are more sensitive, but in most cases the human scent will not stop parents from caring for their babies. This does not, however, mean that it's okay to handle wild baby animals. Babies who are too young to know the difference between you and their parents can become habituated to humans. Habituated wild animals face a lot of challenges when released back into the wild. Some do not survive.

Mallard ducklings swim together in an outdoor pool. Daily access to water is important for mallards so they can develop their swimming skills and maintain their waterproofing. Sunlight is also an important part of their care – without this essential source of vitamin D, or with an early diet too high in protein or sugar, the growth of the birds' bones can be negatively affected.

Babies in Care

T he longer a wild animal is in captivity, the less likely its chances of surviving again in the wild. This is especially true of babies, who can quickly habituate to humans. Wildlife rehabilitators can provide the right nutrition for wild babies to thrive, but they cannot teach them the social skills they'll need to make it in the wild. Most wild babies must be housed with other babies of the same species and approximate age to develop appropriate social behaviors.

They play, fight and cuddle together to learn boundaries, how to defend food and how to recognize their own species.

An orphaned Eastern gray squirrel is hand-fed formula.

Young cedar waxwings crowd together on a branch.

🔍 It's All about the Instincts

As wild animals in care grow, they are offered the same solid food they'll be hunting or foraging for when released. A large part of baby wildlife rehabilitation is providing the correct environment and food, and then stepping aside. It's amazing how quickly a wild baby's instincts kick in. Before you know it, they are digging in dirt pans for worms, swimming after fish and foraging for nuts and seeds hidden in their enclosure. Most important, human contact is kept to a minimum. A rehabilitator knows they've done a good job when the animal they're releasing can't wait to get away.

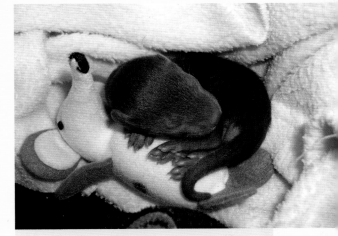

A stuffed toy is a temporary friend for a baby mink while its sibling is getting a checkup.

27

Helping Baby Birds

Canada Goose gosling

Never feed a baby bird unless under the direction of a wildlife rehabilitator. Baby birds need a specific diet and may need to be fed every 20 minutes, depending on their species and age. The wrong kind of food could be deadly.

Rehabilitating baby birds requires special knowledge. To start, it's important to know what kind of bird you're helping. Baby birds fall into one of two categories: they either leave the nest soon after hatching (**precocial**) or stay in nest after they hatch (**altricial**).

Goslings, ducklings and killdeer are examples of precocial babies; they emerge from the egg fully covered with soft down and walk or run within hours of hatching. They might need help if their parents aren't nearby.

Most altricial baby birds (like robins) go through two stages as

Nestling American robins

Fledgling American robin

they grow: nestling and fledgling. Nestlings are still fed by their parents in the nest. When they are old enough, many of these babies flutter down to the ground. These "teenagers" are called fledglings. Although they are out of the nest, they can't fly very well yet and are still cared for by their parents. Fledglings definitely look helpless. They have feathers (little tufts of down might still be sticking through the feathers), but they can't quite get off the ground. They'll mostly be seen hopping around. Because of this, it can look as if they are injured, but they're just learning how to fly. It's important to remember that fledglings are still being fed by their parents and don't need help unless they are sick or injured.

🔍 Reuniting Robins

Toronto Wildlife Centre admitted two baby American robins found on the ground near a cedar tree that had been cut down an hour earlier. The babies were cold but uninjured; there was still a chance they could be reunited with their parents. Rehab staff put the cardboard box containing the babies on a heating pad to slowly warm them up and fed them formula by hand.

A new nest was made by packing an open-topped margarine container with old nesting material and poking drainage holes in the bottom. The container was securely fastened to a tree very close to the location of the former nest and the babies were placed inside. A member of the rescue team waited at a safe distance  to see if the parents would return. Happily, they did. The adult robins accepted their new home and continued to care for the babies.

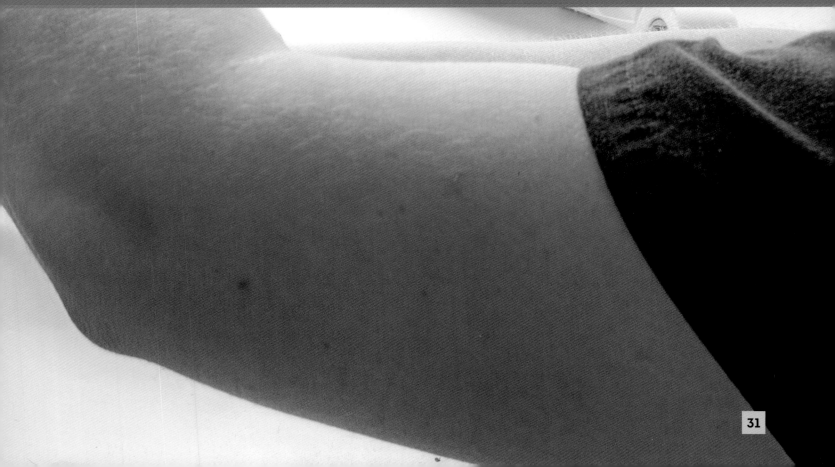

Chapter 3

Life in a Rehabilitation Center

Creativity Required

American woodcock

Toronto Wildlife Centre has admitted over 270 different wild animal species. Some are permanent residents of our area; others are just passing through during migration. Each one has wildly different nutritional and behavioral needs that must be considered.

Take the American woodcock. A fairly common TWC patient during migration, the woodcock uses its very long, thin beak to catch earthworms deep underground. The tip of the woodcock's beak is bendy, like a very stale licorice stick. The bird can move it independently of the rest of its beak to chase after

Baby killdeer

Wild animals must be able to find or catch appropriate foods, recognize and select mates of their own species and escape from predators from the moment they are released. They must also retain their wild integrity (a healthy and natural fear of humans). It's part of a rehabilitator's job to make sure that these things all happen.

worms. In captivity, a woodcock won't eat unless the worms are buried in a container of soil or hidden under leaf litter, mimicking conditions in the wild.

Baby killdeers look like fuzzy golf balls with long, skinny legs. They hide in the wild by huddling under their parent's feathers. A feather duster makes an easy surrogate for these babies when in care.

It takes creativity and expertise to keep any one of the over 270 different species admitted happy while in care.

Enclosures

A sandhill crane improves its muscle condition by being in a large outdoor enclosure.

When wild animals are in captivity, stress management is extremely important. Not only will a stressed animal take longer to recover from injury or illness, but stress can also cause disease. It's scary and confusing for a wild animal to suddenly be exposed to new sounds and smells, especially when they are already weak or in pain. Wildlife rehabilitators work hard to minimize stress levels by keeping contact with humans to a minimum, but also by considering the set-up of each animal's enclosure.

While in care, animals are housed in enclosures that provide them with places to sit, sleep, hide and play. These will differ for each species, which makes it a challenge to get the enclosure just right.

Re-creating Nature

Wildlife rehabilitators must consider the natural history (environment, diet and behavior) of each animal during all stages of wildlife care, including release. Understanding how a wild animal lives in the wild allows rehabilitators to make their life in care as normal as possible.

Rehabilitators add items like rocks, sticks, leaves and branches to animal enclosures. This is called environmental enrichment and is important for reducing the stress levels of animals in care. Each animal is given as natural a home as possible to make them feel safe, encourage eating on their own and allow them to rest comfortably.

An opossum is hard to spot hiding under a pile of branches in his enclosure.

Hiding Out
Wild animals feel safer if they can't see or be seen. Animals in rehab are kept in covered enclosures, behind closed doors or outdoors, only seeing people when there is a medical or rehabilitative need.

Where Am I?

Can you spot the snake in both of these pictures? The picture on the right is an enclosure set up to make a snake feel at home and the one on the left is a lucky shot of a snake hiding in the wild. Leaves and rocks and an extra piece of wood provide plenty of places to hide and feel safe. It doesn't look too different from his natural habitat.

Enclosures

All animals must be safe and secure in their enclosures. Birds can damage delicate feathers in metal cages, so they are housed in soft-sided mesh enclosures or in larger aviaries with vertical wooden bars.

Turtles need heat lamps to bask under, rocks to sit on and water to swim in.

Water birds like mallards need textured mats on the floor of their enclosures so they don't develop pressure sores on their feet.

A young fox explores a large outdoor enclosure. Foxes are curious and get bored quickly in care. Their enclosures have lots of enrichment items to chew and smell.

Some mammals are escape artists. Foxes and coyotes are kept behind double doors to prevent breakouts!

A young opossum hangs around in a fleece hammock. Hammocks, along with boxes, give orphaned opossums options for hiding while in care.

37

Diet

Mallards are dabbling ducks, which means they eat plant matter from the surface of the water or just below it. In care, greens are put in the water for mallard ducklings to eat, mimicking their wild behavior.

Wild animals instinctively know what they should be eating and how to find it. In a natural environment (which is an urban setting for many wild animals), many are opportunistic eaters, taking advantage of food they come across throughout the day. They eat a wide variety of food to give them all the nutrition needed for health and development. Their eating is also seasonal, determined by what is available at different times of year in their native habitat.

Rehabilitation staff must consider many factors when planning diets for animals in care, including natural diet, level of health (animals with broken bones may need more protein to aid the healing process), age (young animals have different nutritional needs than adults of the same species) and how the animal eats.

Getting a wild animal to eat in care can be difficult. They are stressed out, they don't always recognize the food in their dishes as their natural diet, and they aren't used to using dishes! Whenever possible, food is offered to patients in the manner to which they are accustomed. Clover and grass float on the top of duckling pools, skunks dig for their grubs in dirt pans, and

These orphaned cedar waxwings needed to be hand-fed every half hour when they first arrived at TWC. Cedar waxwings mostly eat fruit (even in the winter) supplemented with insects. As they grew, staff added dishes of fruit and mealworms and hung winter berries from branches in their enclosures.

squirrels look for nuts and seeds hidden throughout their enclosures.

Green-Eyed Monsters

How do you make a fussy eater eat? Give their food away! This is exactly what Toronto Wildlife Centre's rehabilitation manager did to six merganser ducklings. The ducklings wouldn't eat, even when offered their natural diet. Recognizing fish and insects as sources of food would be critical to mergansers' survival in the wild. But the ducklings ignored it all.

Several days later, when they still refused to eat, she had an idea.

Knowing that mergansers are extremely competitive by nature, she included a mallard duckling at their next meal. She put all the ducklings on a towel and dropped mealworms onto the towel one at a time. The mallard duckling raced over and ate each worm as soon as it fell. The mergansers didn't like that at all! They soon started to compete for food, even trying to take it out of the mallard's mouth.

The plan had worked. The merganser ducklings continued to eat everything placed in their enclosure and grew healthy and strong, ready for a life in the wild.

An albino Eastern gray squirrel eats a nut she found hidden in her enclosure by the rehabilitation team.

A Skunk Story

 Skunks don't spray without a good reason. If you come across a skunk, don't make any sudden movements. Back away slowly and don't block its exit route. The skunk would much rather get away than spray you. If you have to go into an area where you suspect there is a skunk, make a constant murmuring sound or shuffling noise to alert the animal to your presence.

Skunks like this one have been known to push their heads through the small hole in the top of those domed plastic lids that so often come on fast-food frozen dessert treats. When they finish eating and try to back out, the lid comes off the plastic container, but not off their heads.

When this skunk was admitted to the center, the lid was still stuck around her neck, but also around one leg, forcing it into an uncomfortable upright position. This may have occurred as she struggled

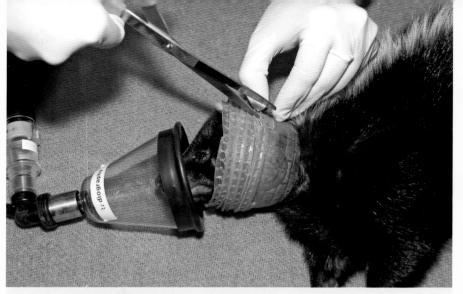

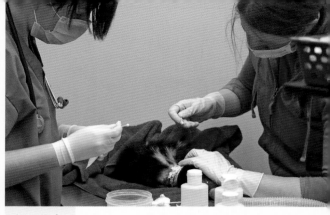

Unfortunately for this little guy, it looks like someone combined seven dessert cups into one before disposal.

A topical antiseptic cream is applied to treat the infected wound.

to free herself. Rendered helpless by the plastic lid, the skunk had not been able to forage for food or find shelter. She was weak and had a dangerously low body temperature (hypothermia). The sharp plastic edge had also caused a deep wound that was now infected.

The skunk was stressed out and the soft tissue damage was severe. To make her more comfortable, she was immediately sedated. The team cut off the lid and examined the wound. The skunk would need stitches, but first the staff would need to treat the infection and swelling with topical antiseptic and anti-inflammatory medication.

Once the infection was under control and the swelling gone, TWC's wildlife veterinarian was able to suture the wound closed.

Much like in a human hospital, the intensive care unit is for animals that require close monitoring for their injuries or illness. For the wild species whose predators attack from above, like skunks (a favorite meal for great horned owls), natural material is placed in the cages for the animals to hide under. This makes them feel more comfortable and reduces stress.

Prevent injuries like this one by cutting up plastic domed dessert lids before throwing them away.

A Day in the Life of a Vet

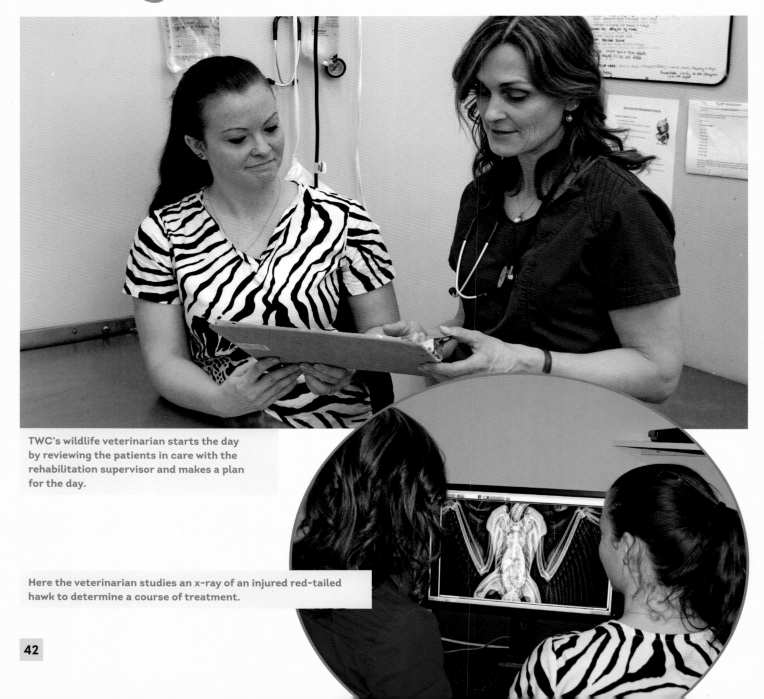

TWC's wildlife veterinarian starts the day by reviewing the patients in care with the rehabilitation supervisor and makes a plan for the day.

Here the veterinarian studies an x-ray of an injured red-tailed hawk to determine a course of treatment.

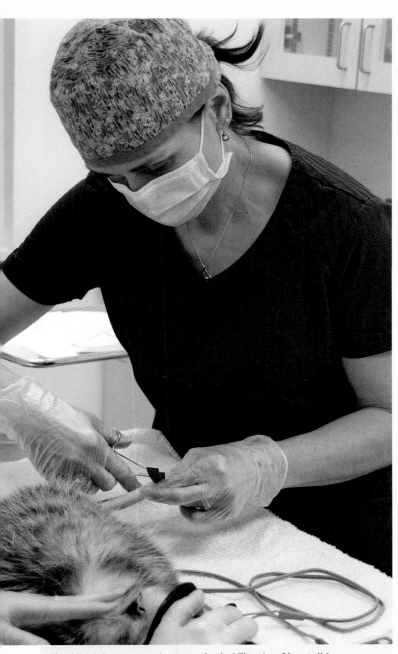

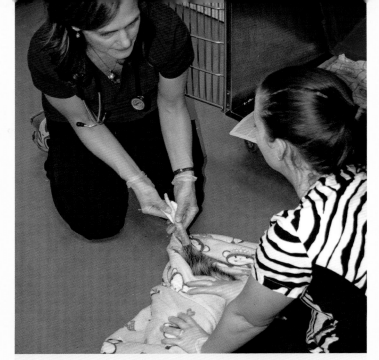

This Virginia opossum has a tail injury and might need surgery. To reduce his stress, they do the examination just outside his enclosure. He is gently restrained while the vet examines his tail. Happily, he will not need surgery and she cleans his wound and applies topical antiseptic before re-bandaging his tail.

This Virginia opossum's not so lucky! The tip of her tail is frostbitten and will need to be surgically removed

Interning at a wildlife rehabilitation center is one of the only ways to receive practical training in wildlife veterinary medicine at this time. The veterinarian shares her unique knowledge with veterinary students by talking them through a procedure.

Raptor Rescue

O n average, TWC admits 25 species of raptors (birds of prey) each year, ranging from huge bald eagles to tiny Northern saw-whet owls. Raptors play a crucial ecological role by keeping the populations of rodents and other wildlife in balance.

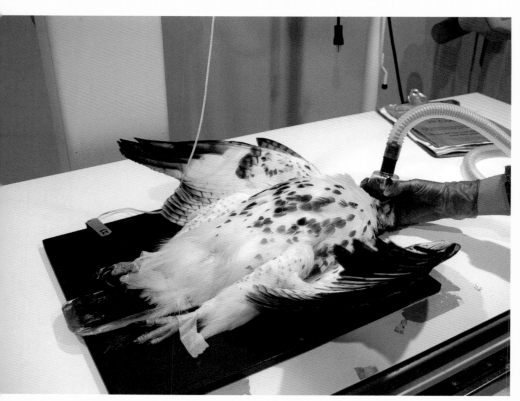

A red-tailed hawk was found lying underneath a shattered window in the backyard of a suburban house and did not fly away when approached. It is not uncommon for red-tailed hawks to fly into windows when chasing prey. Focused on the hunt, they don't notice the glass until it's too late. Hitting a window at top speed doesn't always break the window, but it does usually hurt the bird.

A TWC hotline staff member tells the caller how to safely contain the injured bird by carefully covering it with a box and sliding something underneath. When the bird arrives at the center and is examined, she tries her best to look uninjured. Still, it was easy for the rehabilitators to tell that something was wrong. The hawk was holding one wing in an odd position, and staff could feel what they suspected was a fracture. They administered medication for pain and swelling.

They were right. Her x-rays revealed a coracoid fracture. The

Red-tailed hawks perch in an outdoor aviary.

coracoid is the shoulder bone that helps support wings during flight. She was kept in a smaller enclosure with a low perch to reduce her wing movement and give her bones a chance to heal.

After about three and a half weeks, once her fracture healed, she started a course of physiotherapy. Staff manipulated her wing carefully to increase her range of motion and

rebuild any muscle lost during cage rest. Her final step on the road to recovery was time spent in a large outdoor aviary where she could continue building her flight muscles. This also allowed her to acclimatize to the outdoors. Staff monitored her progress, and when she had regained her full flight ability, she was released.

Raptor Rescue

Two examples of raptor perches. Perches must be tall enough for tail feathers to clear the ground and the right size for the bird's talons. For certain species they should be flat. They must be covered either in rough bark or a textured material to prevent bumble foot (pressure sores).

The rescue team chooses a high point in a large open field to release the red-tailed hawk. Flying from the top of a hill will give her the lift she needs to quickly get into the air.

Chapter 4

To the Rescue!

When sick, injured or orphaned wild animals are in dangerous situations – like high up a tree, down a deep embankment or entangled in fishing line – trained wildlife rescuers are on the job. Toronto Wildlife Centre's rescue team combines years of experience with emergency rescue training.

Not only is this swan trapped in the ice, but has serious injuries caused by a fishing hook.

Common Loon Rescue

Most birds have hollow bones. But loons' bones are solid. This makes them less buoyant, and, as a result, excellent divers. Once underwater, their heart slows down to conserve oxygen and they swim quickly and easily.

Common loons are large water birds. To fly, they need to run along the surface of the water for up to a quarter mile (half a kilometer) before they gain the speed needed for lift-off. If the body of water is too small, they won't make it into the air. And they can't just walk to the next lake. The legs that make loons excellent divers and swimmers are not designed for walking. Because their legs are located close to their back end of their bodies, loons are front-heavy and have difficulty supporting themselves out of the water.

These birds fly long distances during migration and make frequent pit stops to rest and refuel. If they pick a pond that is too small, they could be trapped with little food and in dangerously cold water.

And so, when the center's hotline receives a call about a common loon stuck on a small pond in late November, they dispatch the rescue

The loon is unable to get out of this small pond in the middle of a golf course.

team right away. The team knows it won't be easy to catch an uninjured loon, even in a small lake. Loons can stay underwater for up to a minute when chasing fish. If the bird goes under during the rescue attempt, the team will only be able to guess at where he'll reappear.

Thankfully, the team has a strategy. First, they extend a large net under the surface of the water.

The rescue team sinks a large net under the water to capture the loon from below.

The loon avoids the net floating just below the water's surface.

Because loons are such quick divers and swimmers, catching the bird from below is their best chance. Then they launch their secret weapon: a remote control toy boat. TWC's rescue team isn't just playing around! The toy boat can go where they can't and is used to herd the loon toward the net. The boat does its job. The loon stays far away from the noisy toy, and moves closer to the net and rescue team leader, who had donned an ice rescue suit and entered the water.

But just before the loon swims over the net, he dives. Over the next few hours, this happens again and again, leaving the rescue team

frustrated and concerned. Worried that the net may be too obvious, the team uses a brick to weigh the net down lower in the water, making it all but invisible from the surface. It doesn't help. One end of the lake is now almost entirely rigged with underwater nets, but the loon evades capture.

It's been an exhausting afternoon and the sun is going down, but the team won't give up. They decide to try a loon rescue strategy described in a wildlife manual. Much like deer do when faced with oncoming headlights, loons freeze when a light shines on them in the dark. This technique might just give the rescue

Splash! The loon dives underwater. He could stay submerged for up to a minute.

The remote control boat is prepared for deployment.

The wary loon steers clear of the remote control boat.

Even spending a short amount of time submerged in cold water can be dangerous. The rescue team leader has received training in cold water and ice rescues and his suit will keep him warm and afloat if he has to enter the water.

The team leader enters the water, net at the ready!

team the few seconds they need to scoop up the bird before he can disappear underwater again.

The team leader starts by shining the flashlight on the water to test the strength of the beam. To the team's surprise, the loon starts swimming toward the light. Experimenting, he then moves the beam of light across the water. The bird follows. In this way, they are able to draw the bird close to the shore where he can be captured easily — at last!

Back at the center, the loon is given a full examination and supportive care, including fluids and food. Blood work is done and x-rays are taken to ensure there are no medical problems. The bird is found to be in perfect health, and is given the green light for release.

An Oily Mess

 Ever heard the expression "like water off a duck's back"? Birds preen to lock together the grooves of each feather, which they then cover with a thin layer of oil (that they produce). The presence of the oil means that water beads on contact — as if the bird were wearing a raincoat that keeps them warm and dry. Birds need this waterproofing, as it's called, to survive. Foreign substances can break down this crucial feature.

Images of oil-covered animals are, unfortunately, all too familiar these days. They're synonymous with huge oil platform accidents, tanker catastrophes and even train derailments that spill gallon after gallon of crude oil into our waterways. Spills can certainly be catastrophic for wildlife, but the improper disposal of toxic substances — or even something as

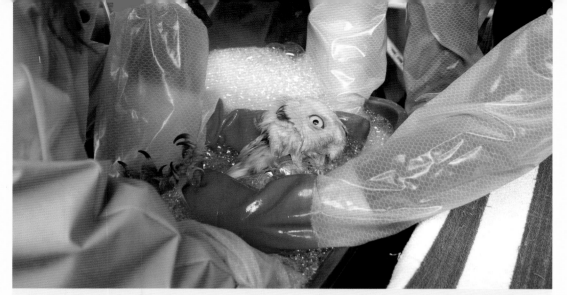

There are many substances that can harm wild animals and therefore need to be removed quickly. This snowy owl was rescued from a sewage treatment plant covered in a pink substance used for processing raw sewage.

Time is of the essence. When a bird preens oily feathers, it ingests the toxic substance and can become ill. Along with washing, oiled animals often need emergency and supportive medical care. Hypothermia and respiratory distress are just two secondary effects of being oiled.

seemingly harmless as cooking oil — can be fatal too. Oily substances can negatively affect wildlife in different ways.

An oiled wild animal will groom or preen in an attempt to remove the strange substance that is covering them, ingesting it in the process. If it's toxic, like crude oil, the animal could be poisoned. But it's not only the toxicity of crude oil that is dangerous for wild animals. Even vegetable oil can be a problem. It interferes with the natural oils certain animals produce and causes digestive issues.

Over the years, wildlife rehabilitators have developed

successful methods for removing oil quickly while keeping animal stress levels down.

Eleven wild animals including this killdeer needed oil spill response treatment after a spill in an urban area. Improperly stored cooking oil had leaked into the sewer system, polluting a small pond where storm water collected.

Saving Swans

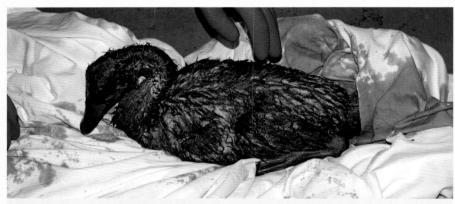

When a mute swan family is found covered in thick, sticky oil, the rescue team catches the parents and their seven babies and brings them to the center for emergency oil spill treatment.

This baby's normally downy gray feathers are unrecognizable.

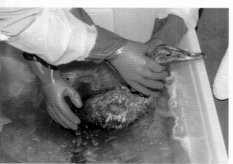

The team sets up the room in advance, filling four buckets with warm soapy water. When the bucket gets too oily, the bird is quickly moved into the next one.

Birds cannot be scrubbed cleaned as their feathers could be damaged. Instead, soapy water is moved over and around the bird to remove the oil.

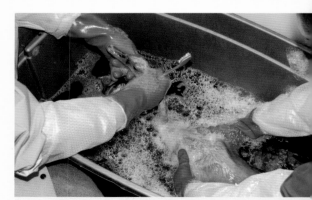

A toothbrush is used to lightly brush the oil from beaks and legs. It can take several hours and multiple washings to properly clean an animal, depending on the severity of the oiling.

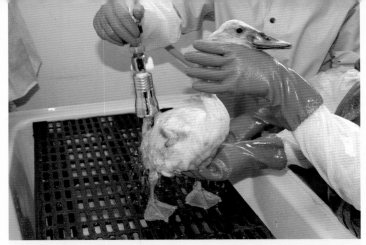
Almost done. A final rinse washes away any remaining oil and soap.

Nice and clean! The first cygnet (baby swan) recovers under the warmth of a heat lamp.

One by one, his newly cleaned siblings join him.

After a week of monitoring and supportive care, the mute swan family is released. The adults slowly emerge from the kennel cabs and survey their surroundings.

The cygnets stay back until their parents give the all-clear.

The family swims away together, wild and free once again.

A just-released fox disappears into the forest. In Ontario, rehabilitated adult wild animals must be released within half a mile (one kilometer) of where they were found.

This orphaned mink was brought to Toronto Wildlife Centre as a baby, but now he's old enough to be released. Careful rehabilitation, including access to natural food sources and limited human contact, has prepared him for life in the wild.

A snowy owl picks up speed moments after his release.

Chapter 5

Release

It seems like this young red fox can't wait to start exploring.

Hardly recognizable as the helpless kit that arrived at TWC, the strong and healthy mink takes his first tentative steps in the wild.

Now that you've learned just how much care goes into the rehabilitation of sick, injured and orphaned wild animals, you can imagine how exciting it is to release them back to the wild. The best "thank you" a rehabilitator can get is to watch as the wild animal they've helped disappears into its natural home without a moment's hesitation.

Making a Difference

R eturning adult female turtles to the wild is especially important. Depending on the species, it can take up to 25 years for a turtle to reach maturity and start breeding, so the loss of a single turtle can

Despite their small size, turtles are completely independent when they hatch.

affect local populations for decades. Breeding female turtles are more likely than males to be killed by cars as they travel to nesting sites.

Turtles play a key role in a healthy aquatic environment by eating plant detritus, dead fish and other animals, which helps to

🔍 Breathing Through Your Bum?

Turtles in more northern climates spend the winter underwater to protect them from the cold and from landlocked predators while they sleep. Turtles breathe oxygen from the air like humans, so how can they stay underwater for so long? And without freezing? This is made possible by a few neat adaptations.

- Turtles are ectothermic. You may be familiar with term cold-blooded, but it's actually misleading. Turtles don't have cold blood; their body temperature is regulated by the temperature outside the body.
- Their very slow metabolism gets even slower in the winter. They no longer use their lungs to breathe and their heart slows down to about a beat every few minutes. As a result, turtles require a minimal amount of oxygen to survive and can get it from the water. And, yes, it's true: some turtle species breathe underwater through their bum via specialized tissues located in their anal vent (they have them in their mouth, too).

keep the water clean. When turtle populations decline, so does water quality, along with the populations of animals that depend on turtle eggs/hatchlings as a food source.

In the summer, Toronto Wildlife Centre's turtle nursery is filled with incubating eggs from turtles that have been injured by cars on the way to their nesting sites. The turtles that hatch will be released in the area that their mother was found.

Turtles are in decline because of pollution, habitat loss, hunting (for food and for the pet trade) and road mortality. And because turtle eggs and hatchlings are excellent sources of food for predators, few will hatch and survive to adulthood. Every hatchling that can be returned to the wild makes a difference to the health of the population and the local environment.

🔍 Snapping Turtle Hatchlings

These tiny snapping turtles hatched in care at Toronto Wildlife Centre. Their mother was found injured by the side of a road and was brought to the center for medical care. X-rays revealed she was carrying eggs, which she laid in a sandbox staff placed in her enclosure. Turtle eggs require a consistent temperature to hatch successfully, and any fluctuations can destroy the viability of the eggs. Using incubators, rehabilitative staff can keep the eggs at the various temperatures ideal for each turtle species and many more will hatch.

Snapping turtles have sharp claws and a tiny hook (called an egg tooth) on the tip of their snout. The hook helps them to break through their shell and falls off within days of hatching.

When the hatchlings emerge, despite looking helpless, they are independent. But to give the young turtles the best chance of survival, they stay at Toronto Wildlife Centre until they get just a little bigger.

Happily, the mother snapping turtle fully recovered from her injuries and was released; her healthy hatchlings followed her back to the wild a month and a half later!

Getting Involved

orking with wild animals is exciting and challenging. If this is a field that interests you, you can look for a school that offers wildlife rehabilitation programs. But the best way to get started right now is to train with a wildlife rehabilitator. Check your local rehabilitators for volunteer opportunities. You might not be able to work directly with animals at the very beginning, but most centers are non-profit and need helping hands. There's always work to be done, and things to learn — including fundraising and volunteer management.

Wildlife rehabilitators must be experts on the wildlife with which they work. Start early by learning as much as you can about the species in your area. Field naturalists clubs and nature centers often put on public walks or hold lectures with wildlife experts.

🔍 Become a Citizen Scientist

Learn about birds and help scientists by participating in your local bird count. In the western hemisphere, the annual Christmas Bird Count (CBC) has asked birdwatchers of all ages and experience to count birds within the same half-mile (1 km) area every year for over a century. No longer only on Christmas Day, local counts happen any time between December 14 and January 5. Volunteers participate in over two thousand locations across North America, Latin America and the Caribbean.

This fun and simple activity helps monitor the population size of an individual species from year to year or the diversity of a species in a given area. Data collected during the CBC is used to monitor the long-term health of bird populations and inform bird and environmental conservation efforts. See the Resource section (page 63) for information on how to find a CBC in your area.

Your local naturalist clubs may offer other opportunities to help monitor and protect wildlife.

Wildlife Rehabilitation Around the World

T here are many wildlife rehabilitation centers active around the world. Here are just a few that are doing good work.

ARCAS

The wildlife of Guatemala is under threat from habitat loss and unsustainable hunting and capture for the illegal pet trade. ARCAS is a non-profit non-governmental organization formed in 1989 by a group of citizens concerned that their precious natural heritage — especially their wildlife — was rapidly disappearing before their eyes. While fairly plentiful even 15 years ago, Baird's tapirs and jaguars are becoming less common. The giant anteater and the harpy eagle have not been sighted in recent years and are presumed extinct in the region. ARCAS was built to rehabilitate wild animals confiscated from the black market by the Guatemalan government. The rescue center is situated on 110 acres (45 hectares) of land on a lake in the northern part of the country and includes a quarantine area, a veterinary hospital and rehabilitation facilities with large flight cages and enclosures scattered throughout the jungle.

LAST

The Latin America Sea Turtles Association (LAST) helps sea turtles through conservation, research, rescue and rehabilitation. With the help of volunteers, LAST patrols

This green turtle has just been tagged by LAST volunteers and is now heading back to the water. Data collected will help conservation efforts to help these endangered animals.

the beaches on the Caribbean coast, protecting the eggs of endangered sea turtles from poachers. LAST's research team also works to assess the threats to sea turtles in the area. Turtles are carefully captured and tagged, and samples are collected before the turtles are released once again into the ocean. Their facility also houses a rescue and rehabilitation center where sick and injured turtles are cared for and eventually returned to the wild. LAST is a member of WIDECAST, an international scientific network with coordinators in more than 40 countries and territories of the Wider Caribbean Region.

Kanyana Wildlife Rehabilitation Centre

This Australian not-for-profit organization is committed to the protection and welfare of native wildlife. Sick, injured, orphaned and displaced wildlife receive medical treatment in their wildlife hospital and are then rehabilitated and eventually released back into the wild. Patients include echidnas, bobtails, quendas, red kangaroos and birds such as the tawny frogmouth and lorikeet. Orphaned babies, such as bandicoots and possums,

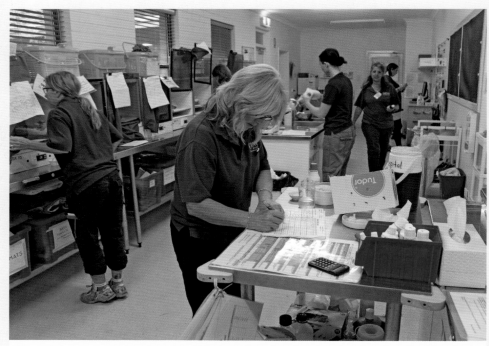

Volunteers and staff members are hard at work taking care of wild animals in ICU at Kanyana Wildlife Rehabilitation Centre.

receive specialized care in the nurseries. Kanyana also runs a successful bilby captive breeding and reintroduction program in response to the declining bilby population on the Peron Peninsula.

Animal Experience International (AEI)

People interested in gaining hands-on experience with animals can volunteer with organizations around the world. Animal Experience International's mission is to help animals around the world by matching clients with ethical, community-based organizations. AEI coordinates volunteer experiences at wildlife sanctuaries, wildlife rehabilitation centers, veterinary hospitals, dog rescue groups and conservation projects in more than 13 countries.

Photo Credits

Resources

United States

National Wildlife Rehabilitators Association (NWRA): *nwrawildlife.org*

International Wildlife Rehabilitation Council (IWRC): *theiwrc.org*

Audubon Christmas Bird Count: *audubon.org/conservation/science/ christmas-bird-count*

Humane Society of the United States: *humanesociety.org/animals/wild_ neighbors/*

The Cornell Lab of Ornithology: *allaboutbirds.org*

International

Hinterland Who's Who: *hww.ca*

Toronto Wildlife Centre: *torontowildlifecentre.com*

Bird Studies Canada (Christmas Bird Count info): *bsc-eoc.org/volunteer/cbc/*

Animal Experience International: *animalexperienceinternational.com*

Index